Superphonics® *Storybooks* will help your child to learn to read using Ruth Miskin's highly effective phonic method. Each story is fun to read and has been carefully written to include particular sounds and spellings.

The Storybooks are graded so your child can progress with confidence from easy words to harder ones. There are four levels - Blue (the easiest), Green, Purple and Turquoise (the hardest). Each level is linked to one of the core *Superphonics® Books.*

ISBN: 978 0 340 80549 7

Text copyright © 2001 Clive Gifford
Illustrations copyright © 2001 Beccy Blake

Editorial by Gill Munton
Design by Sarah Borny

The rights of Clive Gifford and Beccy Blake to be identified as the author and illustrator of this Work have been asserted by them in accordance with the Copyright, Designs and Patents Act 1988.

First published in Great Britain 2001

10 9 8 7 6 5 4 3 2

First published in 2001 by Hodder Children's Books,
a division of Hachette Children's Books,
338 Euston Road, London NW1 3BH
An Hachette UK Company. www.hachette.co.uk

Printed and bound in China by WKT Company Ltd.

A CIP record is registered by and held at the British Library.

Target words

This Turquoise Storybook focuses on the following sounds:

air as in **hair** | **ear** as in **bear**
are as in **dare** | **ere** as in **where**

These words are featured in the book:

air	dared	spare
chair	darling	square
despair	declared	stared
downstairs	Caring	staring
fair	Clare	
Fairy	Clares	bear
hair	glare	pear
lair	glared	pears
pair	hare	swear
upstairs	scare	wear
	scarecrow	
bare	scared	anywhere
bared	scares	everywhere
careful	Scary	somewhere
dare	share	there
		where

(Words containing sounds and spellings practised in the Blue, Green and Purple Storybooks and the other Turquoise Storybooks have been used in the story, too.)

Other words

Also included are some common words (e.g. **said**, **was**) which your child will be learning in his or her first few years at school.

A few other words have been used to help the story to flow.

Reading the book

1 Make sure you and your child are sitting in a quiet, comfortable place.

2 Tell him or her a little about the story, without giving too much away:

Do you know the story about Goldilocks and the three bears? This story is a little bit different!

This will give your child a mental picture; having a context for a story makes it easier to read the words.

3 Read the target words (above) together. This will mean that you can both enjoy the story without having to spend too much time working out the words. Help your child to sound out each word (e.g. **h-air**) before saying the whole word.

4 Let your child read the story aloud. Help him or her with any difficult words and discuss the story as you go along. Stop now and again to ask your child to predict what will happen next. This will help you to see whether he or she has understood what has happened so far.

Above all, enjoy the story, and praise your child's reading!

Turquoise Storybook

The
Three Clares

by **Clive Gifford**

Illustrated by Beccy Blake

Hodder
Children's
Books

a division of Hachette Children's Books

Next to Fairy Wood

stood a square white house.

Three girls, all called Clare, lived there.

Caring Clare was helpful and sweet.

Fair Clare was spoiled and vain.
She spent hours just brushing her
long hair and staring into the mirror.

And Scary Clare was very daring!
She would fight anyone, anywhere!

One day, the Three Clares set off
for the Grand Summer Fair.

"I dare you to go on the Ghost Train!"
shouted Scary Clare.

"If you get scared, I will look after you,"
said Caring Clare.

"Nothing scares me!" said Scary Clare.

"I hope it won't mess up my hair,"

sighed Fair Clare.

(She had spent all morning

preparing for their trip to the Fair.)

Scary Clare just glared.

What shall
I wear?

While the Three Clares were at the Fair,

a bear was standing in their garden.

He had got lost in Fairy Wood.

"I could swear my lair was around here

somewhere," he said to himself.

He looked through the Three Clares' window.

He went into the Three Clares' house!

He picked up some pears.

"A pair of pears!"

he declared.

Bear grabbed another pear.

Then he threw all three pears into the air,

and started to juggle.

But the pears flew everywhere!

Bear tried to catch them,

but he tripped and fell into a chair!

Poor Bear was in despair!

"You should be more careful,"

said a voice.

A hare hopped into the room.

He stared at Bear.

"I love pears!" he said.

"Have you got any to spare?"

Bear smiled.

"Let's share them," he said.

So Bear sat on Caring Clare's chair,

and Hare sat on Fair Clare's chair,

and they ate the pears.

After a while, Bear yawned
and looked around him.

"Is there somewhere I can take
a short nap?" he asked.

"There are three beds upstairs,"
said Hare.

Bear tried out all the beds
before he went to sleep.

Bear woke up with a start.

Voices – downstairs!

The Three Clares were back from the Fair!

"Who's been eating my pears?"
asked Caring Clare.

"It's not fair! Someone's been eating

my pears, too!" whined Fair Clare.

"And who has dared to eat MY pears?"

shouted Scary Clare.

"Who's been sitting on my chair?" asked Caring Clare.

"It's not fair! Someone's been sitting on my chair, too!" whined Fair Clare.

"And who's been sitting on my chair - and BROKEN IT?" barked Scary Clare.

Upstairs, Bear hid under the quilt. He wished he was back in Fairy Wood.

"Maybe I can scare them,"

he said to himself.

Grrrr

He stared into the mirror.

He bared his teeth.

He tried to glare.

"I'm just not a scary sort of a bear,"

he said. "I'd better hide."

"Who's been sleeping in my bed?"
asked Caring Clare.

"It's not fair! Someone's been sleeping
in my bed, too!" whined Fair Clare.

"A BEAR has been sleeping in my bed!"
boomed Scary Clare. "It's full of bear hair!
If I find him, I swear I'll skin him bare!"

Bear was scared.

He liked his hair where it was.

He didn't want to be a bare bear.

He stared at the ground.

It was a long way down.

But he couldn't stay there

on the Three Clares' windowsill.

Time to jump!

Bear sailed through the air.

He landed in the Three Clares' pear tree.

"What are you doing up there!"
asked Hare. "The Three Clares are coming –
there's no time to spare!

Do you see that scarecrow?
Put on his clothes – and hurry up!"

The three Clares looked everywhere.

"Where is that cheeky bear?"

asked Caring Clare.

"I swear he went this way," sighed Fair Clare.

"I'll skin him bare!" howled Scary Clare.

Bear didn't dare move.

"It's not easy, being a scarecrow,"

he said to himself.

When he woke up,

there was nobody there.

He took off the scarecrow's clothes.

"Now I can look for my lost lair!" he said.

"I know where it is!" said a voice.

"Shall I take you there?"

It was Hare!

He led Bear back to his lair.

"Thank you, Hare!" said Bear.

"I never want to eat a pear ...

... sit on a chair ...

... or risk losing my hair ...

... again!"